Pressure Cooker Diet Cookbook

Over 70 Delicious and Easy-to-Cook Recipes for Busy Mum and Dad

By

Olivia Perez

Copyright © 2019, By: *Olivia Perez*

ISBN-13: 978-1-950772-43-8
ISBN-10: 1-950772-43-8

All Rights Reserved. No part of this publication may be reproduced in any form or by any means, including scanning, photocopying, or otherwise without prior written permission of the copyright holder.

Disclaimer:

The information provided in this book is designed to provide helpful information on the subjects discussed. The publisher and author are not responsible for any specific health or allergy needs that may require medical supervision and are not liable for any damages or negative consequences from any treatment, action, application or preparation, to any person reading or following the information in this book.

PRESSURE COOKER DIET COOKBOOK

Table of Contents

INTRODUCTION TO PRESSURE COOKING 6

    Tips before Buying your Pressure Cooker 7

    Tips Before Using your Pressure Cooker 7

    Tips for Cooking with your Pressure Cooker 7

    Safety Tips for Pressure Cooking 8

    Tips for Storing 9

ELECTRICAL PRESSURE COOKER RECIPES FOR A HEALTHY YOU! 10

    Spareribs with Barbecue Sauce-Pressure Cooker 10

    Celery Seed Coleslaw 11

    Pressure Cooker Golden Mushroom Beef Stew 12

    Italian Potato, Rice, & Spinach Soup in Pressure Cooker 13

    Italian Potted Beef-Pressure Cooker 15

    Butternut, Chard & White Bean Soup Pressure Cooker 16

    Oxtail Casserole 18

    Chop Suey Retro 60's Style 19

    Minestrone Soup with Tortellini (Pressure Cooker) 21

    Pressure Cooked Pork Chops 22

    Pressure Cooker Lentil Soup 23

    Flawless Pressure Cooker Brown Rice 24

    Mom's Beef Stew (Pressure Cooker) 25

    Pressure Cooker Split Pea and Ham Soup 27

    Mushroom Risotto in Pressure Cooker 28

    Lamb Shanks with Garlic and Port Wine - Pressure Cooker 29

    Savory Pot Roast a La Pressure Cooker 31

    Pressure Cooker Corned Beef 33

    Chicken Piccata for Pressure Cooker 34

    Pressure Cooker Beef Barley Vegetable Soup 36

    Collard Greens - Pressure Cooker Method 38

Chicken Cacciatore (Pressure Cooker) 39

Pressure Cooker Whole Chicken 41

New England clam chowder (Pressure Cooker) 42

Pressure Cooker Potato and Cheese Soup 43

Pressure Cooker Pot Roast with Mushroom Gravy - Easy 44

Pressure Cooker Italian Chicken and Sausage with Peppers 45

Pressure Cooker Saucy Baby Back Ribs - Fast & Easy 47

Breaded Pork Chops in the Pressure Cooker 48

Navy Bean Soup-Pressure Cooker 49

Sweet BBQ Pressure Cooker/ Grilled Chicken 50

Pressure Cooker - Chili Con Carne 51

Pressure Cooker Jambalaya (With Peppers & Celery) 53

Spareribs with Barbecue Sauce-Pressure Cooker 55

Southwest frittata! 56

Tomato and Chicken Rogan Josh Curry (Pressure Cooker) 57

Pressure Cooker Meatballs 58

Pot Roast Made with Beer for the Pressure Cooker 60

Hungarian Goulash under Pressure 61

Rio Grande Valley Style Carne Guisada 63

Pressure Cooker Chicken Lasagna 65

Fettuccine with Parsley Butter in Pressure Cooker 66

Beef Tips on Rice - Pressure Cooker 67

Flawless Pressure Cooker Brown Rice 69

Chickpea Curry (Vegan -Pressure Cooker) 70

Perfect Risotto for Wolfgang Puck Pressure Cooker 72

New Year's Hopping John 73

Warm Potato Salad with Italian Dressing 74

Amy's Salsa 75

Moroccan Summer Vegetable and Sausage Stew 76

- Brandied Applesauce 78
- Vegetarian Black Beans - 6-Qt Pressure Cooker 79
- Boneless/Skinless Chicken Thighs - Pressure Cooker 81
- Swiss Steak-Pressure Cooker 82
- Quick Parboiled Rice - 2-Qt. Pressure Cooker 83
- Risotto Ai Funghi (Mushrooms) - 2-Qt Pressure Cooker 84
- Pressure Cooker Tomato Lentils with a Kick in 20 Minutes! 85
- Mom's Favorite Dalia for Breakfast 86
- S'more Chicken 88
- Pressure Cooker Brown Rice 89
- Pressure Cooker Ham and Beans with Spinach 90
- Brandied Applesauce 91
- Chicken and Tomato Rice Soup 92
- Thai Chickpeas 93
- Fava Bean Soup 94
- Esau's Pottage 95
- Pressure Cooker Split Pea and Ham Soup 97
- Lamb Chops Rosemary 98
- Corned Beef and Cabbage/Pressure Cooker 99
- Good Ol' Southern Soup Beans for Pressure Cooker 100
- Andy's Spicy Potato Soup 101
- Pressure Cooker Beef Stew 102

CONCLUSION 104

INTRODUCTION TO PRESSURE COOKING

I discovered the joys of pressure cooking when a clever food stylist, stuck for time, ignored the instructions to slow-roast some ribs for three hours and simply popped them in her new pressure cooker for just 30 minutes. The ribs were so tender and it tends to be the best ribs I'd ever tasted and, straight after the shoot, I went off and bought a pressure cooker.

Since then, it revolutionized the way I cook on weeknights. I am very busy like anyone else, but I can now make a stew, casserole or braise meat in under an hour, and a risotto can be on the table in half the usual time, with very little stirring. Remember that speed isn't the only advantage of pressure cookers – they also preserve nutrients and vitamins, as well as being a more economical way to cook.

As compared to the other usual and conventional methods of cooking, food cooked in pressure cookers are able to hold on to most of its vitamins and minerals because it consumes less water and time. Pressure cooker enables you to cook food at half the time up to almost 70 percent faster, all you do is just put all the necessary ingredients and leave it to cook. It gives you the luxury of time to do or attend to other important tasks.

However, you can also expect the kitchen atmosphere to be cooler since the heat is being trapped inside the pressure cooker as compared to other traditional cooking methods.in a pressure cooker you should expect a much cleaner kitchen for food won't be splattering around as it is cooked and sealed in a covered pot.

If you have a big family, I suggest you opt to buy a larger model that could accommodate more than enough. I recommend you buy the **Kuhn Rikon,** this Swiss made, stainless steel, pressure cooker is an excellent example of the newest advances in today's, new modern pressure cookers. They are easy to use, 100% safe, ultra-quiet and loses very little steam.

In addition, pressure cookers are made of stainless steel or aluminum material. So I suggest you go for the stainless steel because of its better cooking results and good quality. And if you do not want the hassle of transferring food from one cooking pan to the pressure cooker, I suggest you opt to buying the heavy duty stainless steel pressure cookers.

If you will be using the pressure cooker for the first time, I will advise you to read first its user manual to ensure safety when using it.

Tips before Buying your Pressure Cooker

You should never buy from flea markets because bargain pressure cookers or older models might have cracked lids or gaskets that don't fit properly. It doesn't have the safety features of new generation cookers – which might mean it can sprout food or even explode when not used the proper way.

Secondly, choose good-quality stainless steel construction as **this is the most durable material used in the market.**

Finally, you make sure your pressure cooker is from a reputable brand with enough replacement parts to repair your pressure cooker.

Tips Before Using your Pressure Cooker

Make sure you read the manual thoroughly before use. This is because different models of pressure cookers have different parts, and therefore, different instructions.

On the other hand, you make sure you check the pot for cracks, dents, and any damage. **And also make sure the gasket is clean and intact, and the steel is flawless.**

Tips for Cooking with your Pressure Cooker

First, make sure you check pressure cooker recipes before you cook your dish. This is because while regular recipes may work for conventional pots and pans, you will need to adjust the time and temperature of your recipes for pressure cooking.

After that, you intensify the flavors of food through browning or sautéing them in regular pans. This is especially recommended for meats and poultry. Feel free to brown your food in the pressure cooker itself but with the lid open.

Make sure you cook with liquid and don't fill the pot beyond the fill line found inside. As for meats, poultry, and vegetables that are steamed, do not go over 2/3 of the pot and not over 1/2 for liquids.

In the other hand, if you added too much liquid and the ingredients are already in the pot, I suggest you reduce the amount by bringing it to boil with the lid open.

When making stew, I suggest you do not add thickeners to the broth or stock when you cook them in the pressure cooker. This is because thickeners like flour and starch will make your dish longer to cook and have a tendency to condense in the bottom. You should add the thickener after pressure cooking.

However, when cooking pieces of meat or vegetables, **always make sure they're uniform-size – this allows for even cooking.**

Finally, beware of frothy foods that may block your vent and valve. Food like this pose a risk for damaging your pot food like oatmeal, applesauce, split peas, pastas, and many others.

Safety Tips for Pressure Cooking

First, you should never leave your pressure cooker unattended for long periods of time. It is necessary to be in your kitchen when steam is let off, as this tells you it's time to lower the heat. And this also signifies that you need to start your cooking timer.

You should never, never force the lid open when pressure is still inside. This is because most new generation models have a locking system that prevents you from opening the lid when pressure is still inside. The older models might not have this safety feature and accidental opening of the lid will burn you.

Always open the lid away from your face to prevent accidents. However, pressure may have been released, there is always a risk for some of the steam to still be present inside.

Make sure you replace the gasket at least once a year to make sure your lid will completely seal-in all steam and pressure.

Finally, placing molds and bowls inside a pressure cooker is easy but getting them out is a challenge; so they're extremely hot and difficult to lift with the limited space.

Before you even put your bowl, I suggest you make sure you can easily lift it out once your dish is done (NOTE: an economical way to do that is by making an aluminum foil sling). You can achieve this by cutting an aluminum foil lengthwise, make sure it is wide enough to sturdily place the bowl in the middle plus 2 handles.

After that, you fold into parts to create a sturdy sling, fold the foil up on opposite sides, and place inside the pot. Then once your dish is done, simply reach for the foil handles and slowly life your bowl.

Tips for Storing

First, you make sure the pot is completely dry before you store it in your cabinet.

And also do not store your cooker with the lid closed. You either place it on the side or place it upside down on top of the pot. Remember that this ensures your gasket or sealing ring won't deteriorate while in storage.

ELECTRICAL PRESSURE COOKER RECIPES FOR A HEALTHY YOU!

Spareribs with Barbecue Sauce-Pressure Cooker

Ingredients Nutrition

Servings 10

Salt and pepper

3 teaspoons vegetable oil

2 cups of ketchup

2 teaspoons of Worcestershire sauce

1 teaspoon of celery seed

10 lbs. of spareribs (cut into serving pieces)

Paprika

4 onions (sliced)

1 cup of vinegar

1 teaspoon of chili powder

Directions

1. First, you season ribs with salt, pepper and paprika.
2. After which you heat canner, add oil and brown ribs and add onions.
3. After that, you combine remaining ingredients and pour over ribs.
4. Then you close cover securely.
5. At this point, you place pressure regulator on vent pipe and cook 15 minutes at 15 pounds' pressure.
6. Finally, you let pressure drop off of its own accord.

Celery Seed Coleslaw

Ingredients

Servings 8

2 lbs. of cabbage (coarsely chopped)

1 cup of shredded carrot

¾ cup of sugar

¾ cup of cider vinegar

1 teaspoon of garlic salt

1 teaspoon of celery seed

Directions

1. First, you mix cabbage and carrot well.
2. After which you mix sugar, vinegar, garlic salt and celery seed thoroughly.
3. After that, you pour over cabbage and mix well.
4. Then you chill.

Pressure Cooker Golden Mushroom Beef Stew

Ingredients

Servings 4

1 ½ lbs. of stew meat

4 carrots (peeled and cut into chunks)

Salt and pepper (to taste)

8 -12 button mushrooms (rinsed and halved)

1 -2 beef bouillon cube (it is optional)

2 tablespoons of canola oil

1 large onion (cut up)

4 red potatoes (cut into chunks)

1 -2 teaspoon of dried parsley

10 ounces of condensed golden mushroom soup

10 -20 ounces of water

Directions

1. First, you heat oil in bottom of pressure cooker until hot and add the meat all at once (**NOTE:** do not turn for at least 1 minute - you really want to let the meat sear)
2. After which you stir the meat, letting it brown on all sides.
3. After that, you add the onions, carrots, mushrooms, potatoes, salt, pepper, parsley, golden mushroom soup, water and optional beef bouillon (NOTE: the bouillon gives a stronger flavor)
4. At this point, you lock the pressure cooker lid in place and bring to high pressure over high heat.
5. Cook for about 15 minutes.
6. Then your cool pot immediately and serve.
7. Remember, if the gravy isn't thick enough then stir a bit of cornstarch to some cold water (only about 1 Tablespoon to half a cup of water) and add to the gravy.
8. Finally, you bring to a boil and the gravy will thicken.

Italian Potato, Rice, & Spinach Soup in Pressure Cooker

Ingredients

Servings 6

6 leeks, white part only (sliced)

2 carrots

3 potatoes (cut in large chunks)

½ cup parsley (chopped)

1 bay leaf

¼ teaspoon of pepper

2 tablespoons of fresh lemon juice

1 tablespoon of light brown sugar

¼ cup of Fontanilla cheese (grated)

¼ cup of olive oil

3 garlic cloves (crushed)

½ cup of Arborio rice

5 cups of chicken stock

½ cup celery (chopped)

1 teaspoon of salt

2 teaspoons of dried basil

3 tablespoons of tomato paste

10 ounces' fresh spinach (rinsed, cut in large pieces)

¼ cup parmesan cheese (grated)

Directions

1. First, in a pressure cooker, heat oil.
2. After which you add leeks, garlic, and carrots and sauté in hot oil 2 minutes.

3. After that, you add rice and potatoes.
4. At this point, you stir well and cook 1 minute.
5. Then you add broth, parsley, celery, bay leaf, salt, pepper, basil, lemon juice, tomato paste, and brown sugar and stir well.
6. Furthermore, you secure lid; over high heat, develop steam to high pressure.
7. After that, you reduce heat to maintain pressure, slide a heat diffuser over burner, and cook 4 minutes.
8. This is when you release pressure according to manufacturer's directions; remove lid.
9. In addition, you stir soup well and ladle into bowls.
10. Finally, you combine cheeses and sprinkle over soup.
11. When you want to serve, serve with hunks of Italian bread.

Italian Potted Beef-Pressure Cooker

Ingredients

Servings 15

9 lbs. rump steak (or better still 9 lbs. chuck roast)

3 teaspoons of cooking oil

3 onions (chopped)

2 cups of diced celery

3 carrots (chopped)

3 bay leaves

1 teaspoon of salt

2 cups of sliced mushrooms

3 (about 6 ounce) cans tomato paste

2 (about 10 ½ ounce) cans beef broth

1 ½ cups of dry red wine

Directions

1. First, you heat the cooker, add oil and brown roast on all sides.
2. After which you add veggies and seasonings.
3. After that, you blend the paste with the broth and wine.
4. Then you pour over meat and veg.
5. At this point, you close cover securely.
6. Furthermore, you place pressure regulator on vent pipe and cook 35 minutes at 15 pounds' pressure.
7. After that, you let pressure drop of its own accord.
8. Finally, you thicken gravy if desired.

Butternut, Chard & White Bean Soup Pressure Cooker

Ingredients

Servings 6

1 large onion (chopped)

3 stalks celery (chopped)

4 sprigs fresh thyme

8 cups of chicken stock

1 teaspoon of fresh rosemary (chopped)

4 garlic cloves (sliced)

4 cups of Swiss chard leave (chopped)

1 cup of crouton

1 tablespoon of olive oil

3 large carrots (chopped medium)

1 sprig fresh rosemary

16 ounces dried white beans

Pepper

2 cups of butternut squash (diced)

Salt and pepper

1 -2 cup of chicken stock for thinning soup

½ cup of sour cream

Directions

1. First, in 1Tablespoon of olive oil, sauté onion, celery and carrot until softened try not to let brown.
2. After which you add in white beans, rosemary sprig, thyme sprig, chicken stock and pepper.

3. After that, you bring pressure to 15lbs and cook for 35 minutes (NOTE: beans should be almost soft but still have a small bite to them).
4. Then using the quick-release, cold water method, open lid, add in butternut squash, garlic, fresh rosemary minced, garlic and salt and pepper to taste.
5. This is when you place lid back on and pressure cook for 10 more minutes with a natural release method.
6. At this point, you stir in chard greens just before serving and use remaining chicken stock to thin soup if too thick.
7. Furthermore, you test to make sure beans are completely soft.
8. After that, you pull out stems of rosemary and thyme.
9. Then you add salt to correct seasonings.
10. Finally, you serve with a dollop of sour cream and croutons.

Oxtail Casserole

Ingredients

Servings 6-8

1 medium onion (chopped)

1 tablespoon of brown sugar

1 (about 6 ounce) of can tomato paste

Beef stock

Salt and pepper

2 -3 oxtails (cut up)

One large carrot

One can tomatoes

2 -3 cloves garlic

Bouquet garni (or a teaspoon of mixed herbs)

Directions

1. First, you brown meat all over in a little oil, in a large pot.
2. After which you add onion and carrot and stir through oil.
3. After that, add crushed garlic, stock, (almost to cover) tomatoes and paste, sugar, bouquet garni and salt and pepper.
4. Then you cook on low for about 2 hours (NOTE: until the meat is falling off the bones).
5. (Pressure cook for 30 mins, or crockpot 8 hours).
6. At this point, you leave to cool, skim off fat; thicken with corn flour mixed with a little water.

NOTE: meat can be removed from bones, just reheat after you take off the fat, and pick up each bone with tongs, the meat will just fall off.

7. Then if it doesn't, it isn't cooked.
8. Finally, you serve with mashed potatoes and greens.

Chop Suey Retro 60's Style

Ingredients

Servings 4

1 tablespoon of shortening

1 ½ lbs. pork or better still 1 ½ lbs. beef, cut in 1/2-inch cubes

Salt

Pepper

Flour

1 large onion (diced)

3 cups celery (sliced)

3 tablespoons of soy sauce

2 tablespoons of molasses

8 ounces' mushrooms (canned reserve liquid)

8 ounces sliced water chestnuts

Bean sprouts, canned (it is optional) or bean sprouts, fresh (it is optional)

Garnish

White rice

Chow Mein noodles

Soy sauce

Directions

Chicken option:

1. First, you sliced some chicken breast thinly and stir fried it then continued with the remaining steps and ingredients using sir frying rather than the pressure cooker (NOTE: Worked wonderfully).
2. After which you heat shortening in cooker.

3. After that, you dust meat lightly with seasoned flour and brown meat in batches in hot, smoky oil.
4. Then you add onion, celery, soy, molasses, and reserved liquids from canned vegetables adding water to equal 1 cup.
5. At this point, you cover and set rocker. (NOTE: The book doesn't specify a setting so I would use 10 lbs.)
6. Furthermore, you heat until you get a steady rocking and cook 10 minutes.
7. Allow to cool, then you stir in vegetables and heat through (NOTE: If you using fresh bean sprouts cook until they are done to your taste.
8. Serve this over rice with chow Mein noodles on top and extra soy sauce.

Minestrone Soup with Tortellini (Pressure Cooker)

Ingredients

Servings 6

1 white onion (diced)

2 carrots (sliced into ¼ inch discs)

8 ounces' dry cheese tortellini (can be found in pasta section of grocery)

1 (about 24 ounce) jar spaghetti sauce

1 ½ teaspoons of Italian seasoning

Shredded parmesan cheese (for garnish)

2 tablespoons of olive oil

2 stalks celery (cut into 1/4 inch slices)

1 tablespoon of fresh garlic (minced)

4 cups of vegetable broth

1 (14 ½ ounce) can diced tomatoes

1 teaspoon of sugar

¼ teaspoon of ground black pepper

Directions

1. First, you add oil to the pressure cooker and heat on high or "brown" with the lid off.
2. After which you sauté onions, celery, carrots, and garlic until onions begin to sweat.
3. After that, you add the remaining ingredients and stir.
4. Then you securely lock on the pressure cooker's lid, set the cooker to high and cook 5 minutes.
5. At this point, you perform a "quick release" to release the cooker's pressure.
6. This is when you check pasta for doneness.
7. If too al dente for your likeness, I suggest you continue to boil on high or "brown" with the lid off to your preference.
8. Finally, you serve topped with parmesan cheese.

Pressure Cooked Pork Chops

Ingredients

Servings 6-8

One small onion

3 tablespoons of steak sauce (or 3 tablespoons of Worcestershire sauce)

Pepper

Carrot (it is optional I personally did not use)

8 center-cut pork chops

1 cup of water

4 -6 medium diced potatoes

¼ cup of butter

Salt

Directions

1. First, you brown pork chops in pressure cooker on both sides (use tongs easier) in ½ of the butter then salt and pepper well (Do NOT cover pan yet).
2. At this point, make sure your potatoes and carrots are already peeled and chunked into healthy meaty portions.
3. On the other hand, have your onion diced into small pieces.
4. After which you take out pork chops with tongs and set aside for a moment while you add the onions and rest of butter to pork fat.
5. After that, you then add potatoes and carrots (if you using) then pork chops add the cup of water and the steak sauce (NOTE: the recipe called originally for Worcestershire sauce but I liked the steak sauce better)
6. This is when you put lid on and lock bring to high pressure once pressure is established put timer on for 15 minutes, then use the regular release method and it is unbelievable a great dinner with so much taste in less than 30 minute (NOTE: including prep if your good with a Knife)

Pressure Cooker Lentil Soup

Ingredients

Servings 4

4 garlic cloves (minced)

2 carrots (chopped)

1 teaspoon of ground cumin

1 cup of dry lentils (rinsed and picked)

Salt and pepper

½ large onion (chopped)

2 tablespoons of olive oil

2 celery ribs (chopped)

4 cups of vegetable broth

2 bay leaves

5 ounces' fresh spinach (it is optional)

Directions

1. First, in your pressure cooker, sweat the onions and garlic in the olive oil until the onions are translucent.
2. After which you add the carrots and celery and sauté for a minute or two.
3. After that, you add the ground cumin and stir well.
4. At this point, you add the vegetable broth, lentils, and bay leaves, close the pressure cooker, and bring up to pressure.
5. Then you cook for 20 minutes.
6. Furthermore, you open the pressure cooker via the quick release method (please see your cooker's owner's manual!) or let the pressure come down on its own.
7. After which you remove the bay leaves.
8. If desired, I suggest you stir in the spinach, and stir until it wilts. (Additional heat is not necessary.).
9. Finally, you season with salt and fresh ground pepper to taste

Flawless Pressure Cooker Brown Rice

Ingredients

Servings 4-6

2 cups of long brown rice

3 dashes Mrs. Dash seasoning mix (original)

Pepper

4 cups of water

4 chicken bouillon cubes

3 tablespoons of butter

Directions

1. First, you spray pressure cooker with cooking oil.
2. After which you add all ingredients to pressure cooker.
3. After that, once pressure is achieved, set timer for fifteen minutes.
4. Then you let pressure drop by its own accord and keep lid on until ready to serve.
5. Remember that this will yield a rice that is not dry, maintains a nice consistency and is far better than any stovetop version.

Mom's Beef Stew (Pressure Cooker)

Ingredients

Servings 4

1 ½ lbs. of rump roast

1 large onion (cut up)

4 celery ribs (peeled and cut into chunks)

Salt and pepper (to taste)

1 -2 beef bouillon cube (it is optional)

1 tablespoon of canola oil

2 garlic cloves (chopped)

4 carrots (peeled and cut into chunks)

4 potatoes (cut into chunks)

1 -2 teaspoon of dried parsley

1 ½-2 cups of water

Directions

1. First, you cut the roast into chunks, about 1 inch (or larger if that is your preference).
2. After which you heat oil in bottom of pressure cooker until hot and add the meat all at once (**NOTE**: do not turn for at least 1 minute - you really want to let the meat sear - this gives the stew such yummy flavor).
3. After that, you stir the meat, letting it brown on all sides.
4. At this point, you add the chopped garlic, stir for 1 minute, then add the onions, carrots, celery, potatoes, salt, pepper, parsley, water and optional beef bouillon (NOTE: the bouillon gives a stronger flavor - you can also wait to see how it comes out, and if you feel that it's not flavorful enough, you can add the beef bouillon and boil the stew for a minute or so).
5. Furthermore, you lock the pressure cooker lid in place and bring to high pressure over high heat.
6. Cook for about 15 minutes.
7. Then your cool pot immediately and serve.
8. ENJOY!

Optional ingredients – feel free to add some chopped tomatoes (if you'd like) before cooking, or after bringing it to pressure, you can throw in some canned mushrooms or frozen peas and heat thoroughly.

Pressure Cooker Split Pea and Ham Soup

Ingredients

Servings 6-8

8 cups of water

1 onion (diced)

2 celery ribs (diced)

Sherry wine (it is optional)

1 lb. of dried split peas

1 small ham bone or better still 1 lb. ham, chunks

2 carrots (diced)

1 ½ teaspoons of dried thyme

Directions

1. First, you fill pressure cooker with water and other ingredients, except Sherry.
2. After which you make sure the pot is no more than half full.
3. After that, you put lid on cooker, place rocker (if model has one) on vent pipe and bring to high pressure.
4. Then when it is at correct pressure start timing for 20 min.
5. Let cooker release steam naturally (**NOTE:** if using a pork bone, I suggest you remove and pull all meat off and add to soup).
6. At this point, you adjust salt to suit your taste at this point.
7. Furthermore, you serve with a splash of Sherry if you wish.

Note: feel free to start this recipe with frozen pork hock by first covering bone with 8 cups water and pressure cook as directed above for about 30 min.

8. Then cold water release pressure and add all other ingredients.
9. Finally, you replace lid, bring to pressure and time for 10 more min.
10. Then you let pressure drop naturally.

Mushroom Risotto in Pressure Cooker

Ingredients

Servings 4-6

4 tablespoons of butter (divided)

2 garlic cloves (minced)

1 ½ cups of Arborio rice (or better still 1 ½ cups risotto rice)

1 -1 ½ cup of fresh grated Parmigiano-Reggiano cheese

4 tablespoons of olive oil

1 medium onion (diced)

8 ounces' portabella mushrooms (sliced)

4 cups of chicken broth

Directions

1. First, in a pressure cooker, heat 4 tablespoon of Olive oil and 2 Tablespoons of Butter.
2. After which you add onion and garlic.
3. After that, you sauté until translucent.
4. Then you add portabella and rice.
5. Furthermore, you stir until rice is coated with oil.
6. After that, you add Chicken broth.
7. This is when you cover and cook under high pressure for 7 minutes.
8. Finally, you release pressure and add remaining 2 Tablespoons of butter.
9. Then you stir in Parmesan cheese and serve.

Lamb Shanks with Garlic and Port Wine - Pressure Cooker

Ingredients

Servings 2

Salt (to taste)

1 tablespoon of olive oil

½ cup chicken stock (or better still other broth)

1 tablespoon of tomato paste

1 teaspoon of balsamic vinegar (up to 2 teaspoons)

2 lbs. of lamb shanks

Pepper (to taste)

10 garlic cloves (peeled and left whole)

½ cup of port wine

½ teaspoon of dried rosemary

1 tablespoon of unsalted butter

Directions

1. First, you trim excess fat from the lamb shanks and season with salt and pepper. **(NOTE:** lamb isn't that fatty, so I didn't trim my shanks).
2. After which you heat the oil in the Pressure cooker.
3. After that, you add the shanks and brown on all sides. (**NOTE:** You can do this in a separate pan if you like).
4. At this point when the shanks are almost completely browned, you add the garlic cloves and cook until they are lightly browned but not burned.
5. Then you add the stock, port, tomato paste, and rosemary, stirring so the tomato paste dissolves.
6. This is when you close the Pressure cooker and bring up to full pressure (15 pounds).
7. Furthermore, you reduce heat to stabilize pressure and cook for 30 minutes.
8. After that, you remove Pressure cooker from heat and let pressure release naturally.

9. Then you remove the lamb shanks.
10. In addition, you return pan to heat and boil the liquid, uncovered, for 5 minutes to reduce and thicken the sauce.
11. Finally, you whisk in the butter, then add the vinegar.
12. When serving, serve the sauce over the lamb.
13. Enjoy!

Savory Pot Roast a La Pressure Cooker

Ingredients

Servings 6-8

1 tablespoon of Season-All salt

1 cup of peeled baby carrots

1 cup of sliced onion

¼ cup of Worcestershire sauce

½ teaspoon of pepper

2 bay leaves

3 lbs. of chuck roast

1 tablespoon of olive oil

1 cup of chopped celery

1 ¾ cups of water

5 medium potatoes (peeled and cut in half lengthwise)

2 teaspoons of beef bouillon powder (or Better still 2 teaspoons beef base)

Directions

1. First, you coat roast with Season All.
2. After which in a non-stick pan **(NOTE**: I use my pressure cooker base for this), brown meat in olive oil, on high, on all sides to sear in juices.
3. After that, you add carrots, celery and onions when meat is nearly browned.
4. Then you add water and Worcestershire sauce.
5. At this point, you place potato halves on top of roast and add pepper, beef bouillon powder and bay leaves.
6. Furthermore, you lock pressure cooker lid in place and bring to pressure over medium-high heat.
7. After that, you adjust heat to stabilize pressure at about medium pressure.
8. Cook for 1 hour.
9. Release pressure naturally (please don't use quick release).

NOTE: As all pressure cookers are different, I suggest you test meat and fork the potatoes to make sure they are done; if not, add water, if necessary, and return to pressure.

10. Finally, when done, release pressure and serve.

Pressure Cooker Corned Beef

Ingredients

Servings 4-6

1 bay leaf

Water

1 (about 3 lb.) corned beef brisket (flat cut preferred)

1 garlic clove

1 teaspoon pickling spices (it is optional)

Directions

1. First, you place corn beef in pressure cooker (NOTE: If, too large, cut in half).
2. After which you add season packet that comes with meat, along with bay leaf, garlic and pickling spices if using.
3. After that, you add water, so just even with top of meat.
4. At this point, you turn burner on, and bring to a boil, put cover and rocker on, and cook until rocker starts rocking.
5. Then you keep at medium to low rocking motion, and cook for 1 hour.
6. Turn off burner and allow pressure to escape on its own (NOTE: carefully open pot and remove meat to serving platter).
7. Finally, you let rest 5 minutes, and slice in thin slices, against the grain with electric knife.

Chicken Piccata for Pressure Cooker

Ingredients

Servings 6 Yield 6 chicken breast

½ cup of all-purpose flour

4 shallots

¾ cup of chicken broth

1 tablespoon of sherry wine

¼ teaspoon of white pepper

1 cup pimento stuffed olive (minced)

1 tablespoon potato starch (or 1 tablespoon flour)

1 lemon, thinly sliced, to garnish

6 chicken breast halves

¼ cup of olive oil

3 garlic cloves (crushed)

⅓ cup fresh of lemon juice

2 teaspoons of salt

1 teaspoon of dried basil

¼ cup of sour cream

¼ cup of fresh parmesan cheese (1 ounce) or better still ¼ cup Fontanilla cheese, grated

Directions

1. First, you lightly dust chicken pieces with flour (it can be easily done by putting flour in bag, then chicken and shaking; excess flour can be shaken off).
2. After which in pressure cooker, heat oil and add chicken breasts, two at a time.

3. Sauté in hot oil until brown on all sides, using long-handled tongs to turn; set aside.
4. After that, you add shallots and garlic and sauté in oil, scraping bottom of pan to loosen browned particles remaining from chicken.
5. At this point, you stir in broth, lemon juice, sherry, salt, pepper, basil, olives and mix well.
6. Then you add chicken pieces' skin side down and secure lid.
7. Furthermore, over medium-high heat, develop steam to high pressure.
8. After that, you reduce heat to maintain pressure and cook for 10 minutes.
9. Then you release pressure according to manufacturer's directions; remove lid.
10. This is when you stir chicken mixture, then transfer chicken to serving platter, and cover to retain heat.
11. In addition, you whisk sour cream and starch together.
12. After which you stir into cooking liquid and cook over medium heat 1 minute, stirring constantly.
13. Finally, you spoon sauce over chicken.
14. Then you sprinkle with cheese and garnish with lemon slices.

Pressure Cooker Beef Barley Vegetable Soup

Ingredients

Servings 6-8

1 (about 28 ounce) can crushed tomatoes

½ cup of barley

2 stalks of celery

1 medium onion (about 6 oz.)

½ teaspoon of dried basil

½ teaspoon of dried rosemary

Fresh ground black pepper

1 ¼ lbs. of lean ground beef

2 ½ cups of water

3 (about 8 oz. total) large carrots

1 (about 10 oz.) large Idaho potato

1 clove garlic

½ teaspoon of dried thyme leaves

½ teaspoon of dried marjoram

¼ teaspoon of salt

Directions

1. First, you brown the beef in the pressure cooker.
2. After which you drain off any fat.
3. After that, you add the tomatoes, water and barley.
4. Then you close pressure cooker and bring up to full pressure.
5. At this point, you reduce heat to stabilize and cook for 10 minutes and while the soup is cooking, split the carrots in half lengthwise, then cut into 1/2" thick slices.
6. Furthermore, you peel and dice the potato

7. After which you dice the onion and mince the garlic.
8. Then when the soup has cooked for 10 minutes, you release pressure and add the vegetables, basil, thyme, rosemary, marjoram, salt and pepper to taste.
9. This is when you close pressure cooker and bring up to full pressure.
10. In addition, you reduce the heat until pressure is stabilized and cook for 10 minutes longer.
11. After that, you release the pressure.
12. Remember that the soup can be refrigerated for up to 4 days or frozen.

Collard Greens - Pressure Cooker Method

Ingredients

Servings 4

½ cup of chicken broth

2 tablespoons of tomato puree (or 2 tablespoons diced tomatoes)

3 garlic cloves (minced)

1 teaspoon of sugar

1 bunch of fresh collard greens

2 tablespoons of olive oil

1 small onion (sliced thin)

1 tablespoon of balsamic vinegar

½ teaspoon of salt

Directions

1. First, you remove the dirt from the collard greens by filling your sink with cold water and soaking them for a ½ hour.
2. Then while the greens are soaking, put the chicken broth, oil, tomato puree, onion, garlic, and vinegar into the bottom of the pressure cooker and stir to combine the ingredients.
3. After that, you remove the greens from the sink one at a time, disturbing the water as little as possible (NOTE: The dirt will remain on the bottom and the greens will float to the top).
4. At this point, you remove the thickest parts of the stems at the base of the greens and chop the stems into small pieces.
5. Furthermore, you place the greens on top of one another and roll them into cigar-shaped bundles.
6. This is when you cut the greens into one or two-inch-wide pieces.
7. After that, you toss the greens and stems with the sugar and salt.
8. After which you add them to the pot and toss to coat with the oil mixture.
9. Remember, pressure cook for about 20 minutes.

Chicken Cacciatore (Pressure Cooker)

Ingredients

Servings 4

3 shallots (chopped)

1 medium green bell pepper (seeded and finely diced)

10 ounces' mushrooms (sliced)

2 cups of crushed tomatoes

1 (about 6 ounce) can pitted black olives or better still 1 (6 ounce) can Kalamata olives, drained

⅛-¼ teaspoon of crushed red pepper flakes (it is optional)

Salt and freshly ground black pepper

1 tablespoon of olive oil

3 garlic cloves (chopped)

½ cup of white wine (not cooking wine)

3 lbs. bone-in skinless chicken breast halves or better still 3 lbs. skinless chicken thighs

2 tablespoons of tomato paste

2 tablespoons chopped fresh parsley (it is optional)

½ cup grated parmesan cheese (or better still ½ cup Romano cheese)

Directions

1. First, you heat the oil in a 4-quart or larger cooker.
2. After which you add the shallots and bell pepper and cook over medium-high heat, stirring frequently, for about 2 minutes until the shallots soften slightly.
3. After that, you stir in the wine and boil until about half evaporates.
4. At this point, you scrape up any browned bits sticking to the bottom of the cooker.
5. Then you stir in the mushrooms and garlic.

6. Set the chicken on top and cover the chicken with crushed tomatoes (NOTE: Do not stir).
7. Furthermore, you plop the tomato paste on top and lock the lid in place.
8. Over high heat bring to high pressure and reduce the heat just enough to maintain high pressure and cook for 8 minutes.
9. Turn off the heat and allow the pressure to come down naturally.
10. This is when you remove the lid, tilting it away from you to allow steam to escape.
11. Finally, you stir in the olives, parsley, red pepper flakes, cheese, and salt and pepper, to taste.

Pressure Cooker Whole Chicken

Ingredients

Servings 4-6

2 tablespoons of olive oil

1 ½ cups water (or better still 1 ½ cups chicken broth)

1 (about 2 lb.) whole chickens

Salt and pepper

Directions

1. First, you rinse chicken and pat dry.
2. After which you season with salt and pepper.
3. After that, you heat oil in uncovered pressure cooker; brown chicken on all sides in hot oil; remove chicken.
4. At this point, you place rack in pressure cooker and place browned chicken in rack.
5. Then you add water/broth around chicken.
6. Furthermore, you place lid on cooker, seal, and bring up to pressure.
7. Cook for 25 minutes, then you release pressure by quick release method.
8. Finally, you remove chicken to platter, pour accumulated juice into bowl and serve with chicken.

New England clam chowder (Pressure Cooker)

Ingredients

Servings 6-8

½ lb. of lean bacon (reserve some for garnish) or better still ½ lb. salt pork, diced

3 cups of raw potatoes (diced, peeled)

¼ teaspoon of white pepper

2 cups of milk

1 pinch thyme (it is optional)

3 (about 10 1/2-14 ounce) cans clams, minced

1 cup of onion (chopped)

1 teaspoon of salt

2 cups of half-and-half

2 tablespoons of butter

Paprika

Directions

1. First, you drain clams and reserve liquid.
2. After which you measure clam liquid; add enough water to make 4 cups liquid and set aside.
3. Then in the pressure cooker, brown diced bacon until golden.
4. After that, you remove bacon and set aside.
5. At this point, you drain off all but ¼ of the fat and sauté onion for several minutes.
6. This is when you add potatoes, salt, pepper and reserved clam liquid (mixed with water) and bring to a boil.
7. Furthermore, you seal, bring up to 15 lb. pressure, reduce heat to stabilize pressure and cook for 10 minutes.
8. After that, you remove from heat, depressurize and remove lid.
9. Finally, you add half and half, milk, butter and clams; heat gently (but do not boil).
10. Make sure you serve immediately.

Pressure Cooker Potato and Cheese Soup

Ingredients

Yield 10 cups

4 small onions (chopped)

1 ½ cups of water

¼ teaspoon of pepper

1 tablespoon of parsley (chopped)

4 (2 1/2 lbs.) large potatoes, peeled and cut into 1 inch cubes

2 teaspoons of salt

4 cups of milk

3 cups of cheddar cheese (grated)

Directions

1. First, you put potatoes, onions, salt and water in cooker.
2. Close cooker and bring to full pressure on high heat.
3. After that, you reduce heat and cook for 3 minutes Remove cooker from heat.
4. At this point, you allow to cool naturally, till there is no pressure inside cooker Open cooker.
5. Then you mix the mixture smooth in a blender or mash it through a sieve.
6. Return soup to cooker; add milk and pepper.
7. Furthermore, you place cooker on medium heat and bring to boil, stirring constantly.
8. After which you add cheese and stir till cheese melts.
9. Make sure you serve immediately, garnish with parsley.

Pressure Cooker Pot Roast with Mushroom Gravy - Easy

Ingredients

Servings 6-8

2 tablespoons of vegetable oil

1 cup of water (or beef or chicken stock)

3 lbs. of chuck roast, 2-3 inches thick

1 (about 1 7/8 ounce) envelope onion soup mix (or better still onion mushroom soup mix)

2 (about 10 3/4 ounce) cans cream of mushroom soup

Directions

1. First, you brown meat on all sides in oil in cooker.
2. After which you mix all other ingredients and add to cooker, coating meat.
3. After that, you cover and cook for about 50-60 minutes after control jiggles.
4. Then your cool cooker normally for 5 minutes, then place under faucet to depressurize.

NOTE: the gravy came out perfect for me -- thin with beef stock or thicken to your own taste.

Pressure Cooker Italian Chicken and Sausage with Peppers

Ingredients

Servings 4-6

4 (about 12 oz. total) Italian sausages

1 (about 4 oz.) medium onion

2 cloves garlic

1 (about 16 ounce) can diced tomatoes

¼ teaspoon of fennel seed

Salt and freshly ground black pepper

1 tablespoon of olive oil

1 frying chicken (skin removed cut into serving pieces)

2 (about 10 oz.) medium green bell peppers

2 tablespoons of red wine vinegar

¾ teaspoon of dried basil

Crushed red pepper flakes

Directions

1. First, you heat the oil in the pressure cooker.
2. After which you prick the skin of the sausages in several places with the tines of a fork.
3. After that, you add the sausages and chicken to the oil and cook until well browned on all sides.
4. Then while the chicken is cooking, dice the onion.
5. Cut the green peppers into 3/4" thick strips and mince the garlic.
6. At this point, when the chicken and sausages are browned, remove them from the pan and set aside.
7. Furthermore, you add the onion, green peppers and garlic to the cooker to cook, stirring often, for about 4 minutes until they begin to soften.
8. After that, you add the vinegar and stir up the browned bits from the bottom of the cooker.

9. This is when you add the chicken and sausages, tomatoes, basil, fennel, red pepper flakes, salt and pepper to taste.
10. Then you close pressure cooker and bring up to full pressure.
11. Finally, you reduce heat to stabilize pressure and cook for 10 minutes.
12. After that, you release pressure and adjust the seasoning.

Pressure Cooker Saucy Baby Back Ribs - Fast & Easy

Ingredients

Servings 4-6

½ teaspoon of salt

½ teaspoon of onion powder

¼ teaspoon of paprika

12 ounces' barbecue sauce

3 lbs. beef back ribs

¼ teaspoon of black pepper

¼ teaspoon of garlic powder

2 tablespoons of olive oil

1 cup of beer

Directions

1. First, you cut ribs into serving pieces.
2. After which you mix spices together to create a dry rub.
3. After that, you apply the dry rub to the ribs.
4. Then you heat oil in pressure cooker and brown the ribs on all sides.
5. At this point, you insert cooking rack in pressure cooker, add beer, and load with ribs, not to exceed manufacturer's maximum fill line.
6. Furthermore, you place over high heat until control jiggles.
7. After that, you reduce heat and cook 35 minutes.
8. This is when you let cooker depressurize naturally.
9. Finally, you remove rack from cooker (you can drain some of the liquid if you like thicker sauce) and add barbecue sauce, heat until simmering.
10. Then you simmer for about 10-15 minutes.

Breaded Pork Chops in the Pressure Cooker

Ingredients

Servings 4-6

Salt and pepper

1 egg (beaten)

½ cup of water

5 -6 pork chops (3/4 inches thick)

1 cup of crushed corn flake crumbs

1 tablespoon of milk

3 tablespoons of oil

Directions

1. First, you season pork chops with salt and pepper Dredge with corn flake crumbs, then dip in egg combined with milk, and again in the crumbs.
2. After which you heat pressure cooker and add shortening.
3. After that, you brown chops on both sides.
4. Then you add water; close cover securely.
5. At this point, you place pressure regulator on vent pipe and cook 12 to 14 minutes with pressure regulator rocking slowly.
6. Finally, you let pressure drop of on its own accord.

Navy Bean Soup-Pressure Cooker

Ingredients

Servings 12

½ cup of vegetable oil

3 lbs. of ham shank

4 carrots (sliced)

¼ cup of minced green pepper

2 cloves garlic (minced)

3 quarts of water

4 cups of dried navy beans

2 teaspoons of salt

2 medium onions (chopped)

4 celery ribs (sliced)

2 cups of tomato sauce

Salt and pepper

Directions

1. First, you soak beans overnight in vegetable oil, salt and water to cover.
2. After which you drain and discard liquid.
3. After that, you place beans and all remaining ingredients in cooker.
4. Then you close cover securely.
5. At this point, you place pressure regulator on vent pipe and cook for 30 minutes at 15 pounds' pressure.
6. Finally, you let pressure drop of its own accord.

Sweet BBQ Pressure Cooker/ Grilled Chicken

Ingredients

Servings 3-4

2 teaspoons of chicken bouillon

½ cup of water

1 teaspoon of cinnamon

2 teaspoons of salt

Bottled barbecue sauce (of your choice)

3 chicken breast halves (bone-in)

1 (about 12 ounce) can beer

1 teaspoon of nutmeg

½ teaspoon of ginger

⅛ teaspoon of fresh ground pepper

Directions

1. First, you combine nutmeg, cinnamon, ginger, salt, and pepper; rub into meat.
2. Then in a separate container combine beer, water, and chicken bouillon; pour into pressure cooker.
3. After that, you place chicken into cooker and cook at 15 lbs. pressure for 20 minutes.
4. Make sure you use the natural release method.
5. At this point, you put the chicken on the grill; cook for 10 minutes.
6. Finally, you brush chicken with barbecue sauce and cook for an additional 5 minutes.

NOTE: it is a little time consuming but worth the effort!

Pressure Cooker - Chili Con Carne

Ingredients

Servings 10

½ cup of olive oil

6 garlic cloves (finely chopped)

3 cups of canned tomatoes (drained and chopped)

1 tablespoon of salt (I used 1 ½ Tablespoons of Mrs. Dash Table blend)

3 tablespoons of chili powder

¼ teaspoon of dried basil leaves

2 cups of water

2 ¼ lbs. lean ground beef

1 lb. onion (chopped)

1 ½ cups kidney beans (soaked)

2 bay leaves

1 tablespoon of tomato paste

¼ teaspoon of pepper

2 teaspoons of ground cumin

Directions

1. First, you divide meat into 2 batches.
2. After which you heat 2 tablespoons oil in cooker for about 2 minutes.
3. After that, you brown and remove first batch.
4. Then you add another 2 tablespoons oil to cooker.
5. At this point, you brown and remove second batch.
6. Furthermore, you add remaining oil (about 4 tablespoons) to cooker.
7. After that, you add onions and garlic.
8. Stir fry until onions are light brown, then you add meat and remaining ingredients; stir.
9. Close cooker and bring to full pressure on high heat.
10. This is when you reduce heat and cook for 18 minutes.

11. Remove cooker from heat and allow it to cool naturally.
12. Finally, you open cooker; discard bay leaves.
13. Make sure you serve hot.

Pressure Cooker Jambalaya (With Peppers & Celery)

Ingredients

Servings 4

8 ounces Andouille sausages (sliced)

8 ounces' shrimp, peeled and deveined (uncooked)

½ teaspoon of dried thyme leaves

1 onion (chopped)

1 green bell pepper (chopped)

3 stalks celery (sliced)

½ teaspoon of dried thyme leaves

1 cup of long grain white rice

3 tablespoons of fresh parsley, minced (or better still 3 teaspoons of dried)

½ tablespoon of oil

8 ounces of boneless skinless chicken breasts (cut into 1-inch pieces)

1 teaspoon of creole seasoning (or essence spice)

1 dash cayenne pepper

3 garlic cloves (minced)

1 jalapeno pepper, finely chopped (it is optional)

1 dash hot sauce (or better still cayenne pepper)

2 cups of canned tomatoes (undrained)

1 cup of chicken broth

Directions

1. First, in an electric pressure cooker, set to browning mode and add chicken, sausage and shrimp.
2. After which you stir well after each addition.

3. After that, you sprinkle meats with 1st amounts of the creole/essence seasoning, thyme and cayenne.
4. Then you cook for 3 - 5 minutes, stirring frequently, until chicken is cooked and shrimp has turned pink.
5. This is when you remove with a slotted spoon and set aside.
6. Furthermore, to the pressure cooker, add onion, garlic, peppers, celery along with remaining creole/essence seasoning, thyme and cayenne.
7. After that, you cook for 4 - 5 minutes, stirring frequently until vegetables are crisp-tender.
8. Then you add rice, tomatoes and broth; secure cover and bring to high pressure.
9. At this point, you cook for about 8 minutes
10. After which you release pressure, remove lid, and then stir in parsley along with cooked meat/fish.
11. Finally, you cover tightly and let stand 5 minutes before serving.

Spareribs with Barbecue Sauce-Pressure Cooker

Ingredients

Servings 10

Salt and pepper

3 teaspoons of vegetable oil

2 cups of ketchup

2 teaspoons of Worcestershire sauce

1 teaspoon of celery seed

10 lbs. spareribs (cut into serving pieces)

Paprika

4 onions (sliced)

1 cup of vinegar

1 teaspoon of chili powder

Directions

1. First, you season ribs with salt, pepper and paprika.
2. After which you heat canner, add oil and brown ribs.
3. Add onions; combine remaining ingredients and pour over ribs.
4. After that, you close cover securely.
5. At this point, you place pressure regulator on vent pipe and cook 15 minutes at 15 pounds' pressure.
6. Finally, you let pressure drop off of its own accord.

Southwest frittata!

Ingredients:

½ cup of diced onion
½ cup of black beans
6 eggs
chili powder, garlic salt, pepper to taste

½ cup of diced red bell pepper

One diced clove garlic

One can, diced potatoes

Cheese
any herbs you may have on hand, for me I used cilantro

Directions:

1. First, you sauté onion, pepper and garlic in olive oil/butter mixture in not stick fry pan till soft.
2. After which you add beans and potatoes.
3. After that, you add herbs and seasonings.
   Beat eggs with fork and add a little milk to thin.
   Once they are cooked through pour eggs over the top.
4. At this point, you sprinkle with cheese.
5. Then you put into 350-degree oven for 20 minutes or until egg is cooked and puffed up and cheese melted.
   Enjoy!

Tomato and Chicken Rogan Josh Curry (Pressure Cooker)

Ingredients

Servings 8-10

140 g curry paste (Rogan Josh we used Pataki's spicy 3 chili rating)

1 tablespoon of vegetable oil

2 large tomatoes (coarsely chopped)

½ cup of coriander leaves (I omitted serve as garnish) (it is optional)

390 g Greek yogurt (or better still 1 ½ cups Greek yogurt)

2 ¼ kg boneless skinless chicken thighs (trimmed of fat and I cut each into 3 pieces)

1 onion (preferably brown large cut into wedges)

100 g baby spinach leaves (I prefer silver beet sliced)

Directions

1. First, you combine the yoghurt and curry paste in a large glass or ceramic bowl (NOTE: I ended up using stainless steel as it was the only bowl that was big enough) and then add the chicken to coat and cover with plastic wrap and place into the fridge for 30 minutes to marines (NOTE: mine was in for nearly 1 1/2 hours).
2. After which you heat oil in the pressure cooker (NOTE: though I did it in a separate fry pan as I was making ahead but use the pressure cooker if you are going to be cooking the chicken straight away) and add onion and cook until golden, this took me about 10 minutes but I had wedges of onion, if thinly sliced would take about 3 to 5 minutes.
3. After that, you add the cooked onion and diced tomatoes to your marinated chicken mix and place in the pressure cooker, (NOTE: at this point I used an electric pressure cooker, I sealed in the pressure cooker and set the timer for high pressure for 15 minutes, it took 18 minutes to come up to pressure and then cooked for 15 minutes and then did fast release)
4. Then you served over rice and with steamed vegetables and Nan bread on the side.

Pressure Cooker Meatballs

Ingredients

Servings 4

½ cup of milk

8 ounces of ground pork

1 small onion (minced)

1 tablespoon of dried oregano

¼ cup of butter

0.75 (about 14 ounce) can chicken stock, diluted with equal amount of water (remember you can sub homemade beef broth for the chicken broth)

Salt (to taste)

Herbs, garnish (preferably parsley, fresh herbs anything you like to add some color)

1 slice of whole wheat bread

1 lb. of extra lean ground beef

1 egg

1 ½ tablespoons of dried thyme

½ teaspoon of salt

¼ cup of all-purpose flour

½ cup of whipping cream

Pepper (to taste)

Cooked egg noodles

Directions

1. First, in a large bowl, soak bread in milk until absorbed.
2. After which you use your hands, break up bread; mix in beef and pork.
3. After that, you stir in egg, minced onion, thyme, oregano and salt.

4. Then you form into 3/4 inch (2 cm) balls (NOTE: this is often a smaller size than you think!) Set aside.
5. Furthermore, in a pressure cooker, melt butter over medium-high heat; stir in flour until moistened.
6. After that, you gradually whisk in beef broth and water.
7. At this point, you bring to a simmer and carefully transfer meatballs to sauce.
8. This is when you lock the lid in place and bring cooker up to full pressure over medium -high heat.
9. In addition, you reduce to medium-low, just to maintain even pressure, and cook for 10 minutes.
10. After which you remove from heat and release pressure quickly.
11. Then you stir in cream and simmer until sauce is creamy and thick.
12. Finally, you season to taste with salt and pepper.
13. When serving, serve over cooked egg noodles, sprinkled with garnish of choice.

Pot Roast Made with Beer for the Pressure Cooker

Ingredients

Servings 4-6

3 tablespoons of olive oil

1 teaspoon of paprika

½ teaspoon of black pepper

2 tablespoons of flour

1 cup of beef broth (or chicken)

6 carrots

1 ½-2 lbs. of chuck roast

2 tablespoons of mustard

½ teaspoon of coarse salt

12 ounces of beer

2 tablespoons of tomato paste

1 large onion

Directions

1. First, you heat oil in pressure cooker (medium).
2. After which you brown beef on both sides, then remove and set aside.
3. After that, you add to same pan: small amount of beer and loosen/stir up bits.
4. At this point, you add flour and tomato paste to pan and cook over medium for one minute.
5. Then you place the meat and everything else (and the rest of the beer) in the pan.
6. This is when you close lid and cook on high pressure for about 1 hour.
7. Finally, you let pressure come down naturally.
8. When serving, serve over rice or noodles.

Hungarian Goulash under Pressure

Ingredients

Servings 6

1 tablespoon of unsalted butter

2 large onions (about 1 lb.)

2 medium green bell peppers

3 tablespoons of tomato paste

Salt and pepper

1 ½ teaspoons of caraway seeds

2 ounces of salt pork

2 lbs. of beef, ramp cut into 1 1/2 inch cubes

6 small red potatoes

½ cup of dry white wine

4 teaspoons of Hungarian paprika

1 cup of sour cream

Directions

1. First, you dice the salt pork.
2. After which you melt the butter in the pressure cooker.
3. After that, you add the salt pork and cook until brown and crisp.
4. At this point, you add the beef and brown lightly on all sides.
5. In the meantime, peel the onions and cut them into wedges.
6. Then you peel the potatoes and cut in half.
7. Cut the green peppers into 1" squares and add the onions, potatoes, and green peppers to the pan.
8. Furthermore, you stir together the wine, tomato paste, paprika and salt and pepper to taste and add to the pressure cooker.
9. After which you cover pressure cooker and bring up to full pressure.
10. After that, you reduce heat to stabilize pressure and cook for about 12 minutes.
11. Release pressure and stir in the sour cream and caraway.

12. Finally, you serve hot topped with additional sour cream, if desired.
13. Remember that this goulash can be made in advance and refrigerated or frozen.

Rio Grande Valley Style Carne Guisada

Ingredients

Servings 4

1 tablespoon of vegetable oil

¼ teaspoon of dried oregano leaves

1 teaspoon of fresh ground black pepper

1 clove garlic (minced)

½ onion (sliced)

½ cup of tomato sauce

1 teaspoon of paprika

2 tablespoons of vegetable oil

1 ½ lbs. round steaks

3 cups of water

1 teaspoon of cumin seed

1 ½ teaspoons of salt

½ green bell pepper (diced)

One fresh tomato (diced)

1 tablespoon of chili powder

2 teaspoons of all-purpose flour

Directions

1. First, you cube meat (about 1"), removing all fat and gristle.
2. After which you sear meat in oil.
3. After that, you add water and cook on medium-low heat for about 30 minutes, stirring occasionally.

4. At this point, you toast cumin seeds in a small sauté skillet on medium-high until they begin to smoke slightly.
5. Then you grind the hot cumin seeds with a mortar and pestle.
6. Furthermore, you add oregano, ground toasted cumin, black pepper, salt and garlic to the meat.
7. After that, you add vegetables (bell pepper, onion and tomato) and continue to cook about 30 minutes.
8. This is when you add tomato sauce, chili powder and paprika.
9. Then you continue to simmer for another 15-20 minutes.
10. While the meat is simmering, I suggest you heat 2 tablespoons of oil in a small sauté pan and add flour over medium-low heat.
11. In addition, you stir the flour and oil constantly until the flour turns a light golden brown (roux).
12. After which you add the roux to the meat and continue to simmer for about another 30 minutes.
13. Finally, you serve carne guisada with rice and beans and flour or corn tortillas.

Note: you can speed the cooking time by using a pressure cooker.

Pressure Cooker Chicken Lasagna

Ingredients

Servings 4-6

400 g frozen spinach

1 tablespoon of butter

½ teaspoon of nutmeg

3 large tomatoes (sliced)

200 g no-boil lasagna noodles

1 kg of cooked chicken (I prefer my pressure cooker chicken recipe)

Sauce

2 tablespoons of flour

2 -3 cups chicken stock

200 g of cheese (grated)

Directions

1. Meanwhile, heat oven to 180°C (355°F).
2. After which you make the sauce by melting the butter over a low heat.
3. After that, you add the flour and nutmeg and then all but a few Tablespoons of the chicken stock.
4. Then you stir until thickened, set aside to cool slightly.
5. At this point, you drizzle the chicken stock that you reserved into the bottom of a 23 x 23 cm (9 x 9 inch) high sided oven dish.
6. This is when you layer some of the dry, no boil lasagna noodles on top of this (**NOTE:** I prefer layers 2-3 sheets thick).
7. You layer in the following order repeatedly until you have used all ingredients, (**NOTE:** the last layer should be grated cheese).
8. In addition, shredded cooked chicken, then some of the mushed vegetables, spinach, tomato (if using) more noodles, then sauce and cheese.
9. Finally, you bake for about 40 minutes until top is golden brown and lasagna noodles are cooked.

Fettuccine with Parsley Butter in Pressure Cooker

Ingredients

Servings 6

½ lb. of fettuccine pasta

1 teaspoon of salt

½ teaspoon of dried summer savory, crushed

¼ cup of Fontanilla cheese, grated (or Parmesan cheese)

2 tablespoons of olive oil

3 cups of chicken broth

¼ teaspoon of white pepper

¼ cup butter (softened)

¼ cup fresh parsley (chopped)

Directions

1. First, in a pressure cooker, heat oil and stir fettuccine into hot oil.
2. After which you add broth, salt, pepper, and savory.
3. Secure lid and over high heat, develop steam to HIGH PRESSURE.
4. After that, you reduce heat to maintain pressure and cook for 8 minutes.
5. At this point, you release pressure according to manufacturer's directions.
6. Then you remove lid.
7. Furthermore, you drain fettuccine through a colander and return to cooker.
8. After that, you add butter and parsley, mixing gently until fettuccine is well coated.
9. Finally, you pour into a serving bowl and sprinkle with cheese.
10. Makes about 6 servings.

Beef Tips on Rice - Pressure Cooker

Ingredients

Servings 4-6 Yield 4

2 teaspoons of salt

½ teaspoon of paprika

2 lbs. of top sirloin steaks (cut into cubes)

2 onions (chopped)

4 cups of cooked rice

3 tablespoons of all-purpose flour

½ teaspoon of black pepper

¼ teaspoon of mustard powder

2 tablespoons of vegetable oil

2 garlic cloves (minced)

1 (about 10 ½ ounce) can beef consommé

Directions

1. First, you place the all-purpose flour, salt, black pepper, paprika and mustard powder in a zip top bag and shake well to distribute.
2. After which you add the beef cubes to the bag and shake until all are well covered.
3. Then in a pressure cooker, brown the meat in the vegetable oil over medium heat.
4. At this point, once the meat is browned, add the onions and the garlic to the cooker and sauté the onions while deglazing the pan.
5. Furthermore, once the onions turn translucent add the can of beef consommé and stir to combine.
6. After that, you place the lid on the cooker and bring to pressure over medium heat.
7. Cook for about 25 minutes and remove from heat.

8. Finally, once the pressure subsides open the lid and simmer until the proper consistency.
9. When serving, I suggest you serve over rice.

Flawless Pressure Cooker Brown Rice

Ingredients

Servings 4-6

2 cups of long brown rice

3 dashes of Mrs. Dash seasoning mix (original)

Pepper

4 cups of water

4 chicken bouillon cubes

3 tablespoons of butter

Directions

1. First, you spray pressure cooker with cooking oil.
2. After which you add all ingredients to pressure cooker.
3. Then once pressure is achieved, set timer for fifteen minutes.
4. Finally, you let pressure drop by its own accord and keep lid on until ready to serve.

NOTE: This will yield a rice that is not dry, maintains a nice consistency and is far better than any stovetop version.

Chickpea Curry (Vegan -Pressure Cooker)

Ingredients

Servings 6

4 teaspoons of cumin seeds

4 teaspoons of crushed garlic (extra if you want more garlic flavor)

2 teaspoons of garam masala (extra for a spicier dish)

3 cups of cooked chickpeas (roughly 29.5 ounces in total) or 2 (420 g) cans chickpeas, rinsed well and drained (roughly 29.5 ounces in total)

3 large potatoes (peeled and cut into cubes)

¼ teaspoon of fresh ground black pepper

Fresh cilantro stem, as garnish (cilantro also known as coriander)

8 teaspoons of olive oil

1 large onion (finely sliced)

2 teaspoons of ground coriander

2 teaspoons of ground turmeric

2 (about 400 g) cans diced tomatoes (roughly 28 ounces in total)

¼ teaspoon of salt (feel free to add more to taste if desired)

½ cup of water

Garnish

Directions

1. First, you heat the oil in the pressure cooker over high heat.
2. After which you cook the cumin seeds for approx. 30 seconds or until they start to crackle.
3. After that, you add the sliced onion and cook, stirring, for 5 minutes (NOTE: The onion should be golden and soft).
4. At this point, you reduce the heat and stir in the garlic and other spices.
5. Then you add all remaining ingredients (except garnish).

6. Furthermore, you close and lock the lid.
7. After which you bring to high pressure over high heat.
8. This is when you reduce heat to stabilize the pressure and cook for 15 minutes.
9. Finally, you release pressure and serve with a sprig of coriander or a sprinkle of parsley.
10. Then serve with steamed basmati rice, naan or pappadums.

NOTE: if you want to cook dried beans, I suggest you overnight soak, drain water, place into pressure cooker, cover with fresh water and cook on low pressure for 10 minutes. For me I soaked 2 cups of dried chickpeas and result was a little over 4 cups cooked beans. You can use canned/tinned chickpeas, if desire (NOTE: be sure to drain and wash them well).

Perfect Risotto for Wolfgang Puck Pressure Cooker

Ingredients

Servings 6

1 medium onion (finely chopped)

3 ½ cups of chicken stock

1 -3 tablespoon of Romano cheese or better still 1 -3 tablespoon parmesan cheese (for finishing)

1 -2 tablespoon of olive oil

1 ½ cups of Arborio rice

Black pepper (to taste for finishing)

Directions

1. First, you heat oil in cooker using the vegetable function.
2. After which you add onion and sauté until tender and translucent.
3. After that, you add rice and stock.
4. Then you lock lid in place.
5. At this point, you select rice function and set timer for about 15 minutes.
6. Furthermore, when cycle is done and all pressure has been released, open lid.
7. Finally, you stir in black pepper to taste and 1 - 3 tablespoons of Romano or parmesan cheese, also to taste.
8. Make sure you serve immediately.

New Year's Hopping John

Ingredients

Servings 6 Yield 12 side dish serving

One medium onion

One tablespoon oil, bacon drippings (or 1 tablespoon butter)

2 (about 10 1/2 ounce) cans chicken broth (or 2 ½ cups)

½ lb. of cooked ham (cubed)

3 cups of cooked long-grain rice

1 cup of sliced celery

2 cloves garlic (minced)

4 cups of water

16 ounces black-eyed peas (preferably fresh or frozen, thawed)

¼ teaspoon of dry crushed red pepper

3 bay leaves

Directions

1. First, you sauté the sliced celery, onion and garlic in a large Dutch oven in hot oil, bacon drippings, or butter until tender.
2. After which you add water, oil, chicken broth, black-eyed peas and ham.
3. After that, you bring to a boil; cover, reduce heat, and simmer for 40 minutes or until peas are tender.
4. Then you remove and discard bay leaf.
5. Finally, you serve over rice

Warm Potato Salad with Italian Dressing

Ingredients

Servings 6

180 ml of light Italian dressing

5 g parsley (chopped)

1 ½ yellow bell peppers (seeded and finely diced)

Black pepper

680 g of small red potatoes (scrubbed)

5 shallots (finely sliced)

1 ½ red bell peppers (seeded and finely diced)

½ teaspoon of salt, to taste (it is optional)

Directions

1. First, you boil whole potatoes in salted water for 20 minutes or until tender.
2. Drain and rinse under cold water until just cool enough to handle.
3. After which you drain again.
4. After that, you cut potatoes into 1.5 cm pieces and place in a salad bowl.
5. Then you add the remaining ingredients and pepper to taste to the potatoes.
6. Finally, you toss lightly and serve with a warm smile.

Amy's Salsa

Ingredients

Yield 6 pint jars

24 ounces of tomato paste

5 garlic cloves

2 -3 green peppers

¼ cup of cilantro

16 cups of tomatoes (peeled and seeded)

5 onions (chopped)

2 -3 jalapeno peppers

2 teaspoons of kosher salt

1 cup of vinegar

Directions

1. First, you add all ingredients into a large pan.
2. After which you simmer for 30 minutes.
3. After that, you pour into canning jars put the lids and rings on and process the method you like best.

NOTE: I just HOT packed the salsa into HOT jars with HOT lids put the ring on and they all sealed. PING PING PING we were done.

Moroccan Summer Vegetable and Sausage Stew

Ingredients

Servings 8

2 cups of chopped onions

5 cups of cubed eggplants (about 3/4 inch cubes)

1 cup of fat-free chicken broth

1 tablespoon of ground coriander

¼-½ teaspoon of crushed red pepper flakes

1 (about 15 1/2 ounce) can chickpeas (rinsed and drained)

⅓ cup of golden raisin

1 cup of crumbled feta cheese

2 teaspoons of olive oil

1 lb. of hot Italian turkey sausage

4 cups of yellow onions (coarsely chopped)

1 tablespoon of ground cumin

½ teaspoon of salt

4 garlic cloves (minced)

1 (about 14 1/2 ounce) can diced tomatoes, undrained

3 tablespoons of fresh thyme, chopped

6 cups of hot cooked couscous

Directions

1. First, you heat the oil in a 6-quart pressure cooker over medium-high heat.
2. After which you add in the onion; stir/sauté for about 2 minutes.
3. After that, you add in the sausage; stir/sauté for 2 minutes (stir to crumble).
4. Then you add in eggplant, yellow onions, chicken broth, ground cumin, ground coriander, salt, red pepper flakes, garlic cloves, chickpeas and tomatoes; stir to combine.
5. At this point, you close lid securely; bring to high pressure over high heat.

6. Furthermore, you adjust heat to medium or level needed to maintain high pressure; cook for 4 minutes.
7. After that, you remove cooker from heat and place under cold running water.
8. Finally, you remove lid and stir in raisins and thyme.
9. Finally, you serve stew over couscous and top with crumbled cheese.

Brandied Applesauce

Ingredients

Servings 10 Yield 5 cups

¾ cup of dark brown sugar

⅓ cup of brandy (preferable applejack)

1 pinch of nutmeg

1 pinch of ground ginger

½ tablespoon of lemon zest (about 1/2 lemon)

4 lbs. granny smith apples

½ cup of apple cider

2 cinnamon sticks

1 pinch of ground cloves

1 ½ tablespoons of fresh lemon juice (about 1/2 lemon)

Directions

1. First, you peel, core, and quarter the apples.
2. Then in a pressure cooker, combine all the ingredients and cook at high pressure for 2 minutes.
3. After which you let pressure release naturally (NOTE: it'll take 10 to 20 minutes), then remove cinnamon sticks and coarsely chop the apples; alternatively, puree the apples if you prefer a smoother texture.
4. After that, you taste and adjust sweetness and flavorings.
5. Finally, you set aside to cool, then cover and refrigerate.

Vegetarian Black Beans - 6-Qt Pressure Cooker

Ingredients

Servings 16-18 Yield 8-9 cups

One medium onion, finely chopped (110g)

½ teaspoon of salt

1 lb. (about 2 1/3 cups) dried black beans, picked over and rinsed but not soaked

3 tablespoons of olive oil

8 cups of water

ADD WHEN REHEATING

¼ cup of cream sherry (or ¼ cup medium-dry sherry)

1 teaspoon of salt

1 -2 tablespoon of soy sauce

1 -2 tablespoon of balsamic vinegar

Directions

1. First, in a 6- to 8-quart pressure cooker, combine beans, onion, oil, water and ½ teaspoon salt.
2. After which you seal pressure cooker with lid and cook at high pressure, according to manufacturer's directions, for about 30-45 minutes until beans are tender.
3. After that, you remove from heat.
4. Then you use quick release method favored by your manufacturer; put the pressure cooker in the sink (with lid still attached) and run cold water over the lid until pressure goes down completely.

NOTE: Don't try the cold water method with an electric pressure cooker!

5. Finally, you chill uncovered until completely cooled, then chill, covered, up to 1 week or freeze up to 3 months.

REHEATING.

1. Remember, when reheating the beans later, stir in Sherry, 1 teaspoon salt, then soy sauce and vinegar to taste (start with 1 tablespoon each).

2. After which you thin with water if necessary.
3. Then you simmer, uncovered, stirring occasionally, for 5 minutes.

Boneless/Skinless Chicken Thighs - Pressure Cooker

Ingredients

Yield 4 thighs

1 cup of water

4 -12 boneless skinless chicken thighs

Directions

1. First, you add water to pressure cooker.
2. After which you add chicken and bring cooker to high pressure.
3. After that, you hold at high pressure for about 10 - 12 minutes.
4. At this point, you carefully quick release pressure.
5. Finally, you check for doneness.

Swiss Steak-Pressure Cooker

Ingredients

Servings 24

1 cup of flour

4 teaspoons of cooking oil

4 cups of tomato juice

12 lbs. round steaks (about 1-inch-thick cut into serving pieces)

Salt and pepper

2 onions (chopped)

4 green peppers (chopped)

Directions

1. First, you season flour with salt and pepper, pound flour into beef.
2. After which you heat cooker and add oil, brown meat.
3. After that, you add remaining ingredients.
4. Then you close cover securely.
5. At this point, you place pressure regulator on vent pipe and cook for 15 minutes at 15 pounds' pressure.
6. Finally, you let pressure drop of its own accord.

Quick Parboiled Rice - 2-Qt. Pressure Cooker

Ingredients

Servings 6 Yield 3 cups

1 cup of parboiled rice (rinsed and drained)

1 ½ cups of water

Directions

1. First, in pressure cooker, pour in water and bring it to a rolling boil.
2. After which you pour in well-drained rice, stir well.
3. After that, you secure lid, and bring to low pressure (8 psi).
4. Then once pot has reached low pressure, adjust heat to stabilize at low pressure. (NOTE: My stove runs hot for a simmer, so I press the steam valve of my Kuhn Rikon pressure cooker lid to keep the pressure at 1 bar.)
5. Furthermore, once low pressure has been reached, begin timing for 6 minutes and cook for 6 minutes.
6. After which you remove from heat.
7. At this point, you let pressure reduce naturally (remember that this will absorb some of the excess water, if any).
8. Finally, you remove lid, and serve.

Risotto Ai Funghi (Mushrooms) - 2-Qt Pressure Cooker

Ingredients

Servings 4-6

1 medium onion (peeled and finely chopped)

1 cup of fresh mushrooms, chopped or better still ¼ cup dried porcini mushrooms, chopped and soaked to rehydrate

¼ cup of sun-dried tomato (chopped and soaked to rehydrate)

¼ cup of parmesan cheese (grated)

1 tablespoon of olive oil

1 cup of Arborio rice

¼ cup of dry white wine

2 cups of chicken broth (or better still 2 cups vegetable broth)

2 tablespoons of fresh rosemary (or to taste) or better still 2 tablespoons fresh basil (or to taste) or 2 tablespoons fresh thyme, finely chopped (or to taste)

Directions

1. First, in a 2-quart Pressure Fry pan or larger pressure cooker, heat olive oil over medium-high heat.
2. After which you add onion and sauté until translucent.
3. After that, you add rice, stirring often, until lightly golden.
4. Add mushrooms and stir to mix.
5. Add wine and stir to mix.
6. In addition, you add tomatoes, broth and stir to mix.
7. At this point, you increase heat to high.
8. Stir in fresh herb of choice and continue to stir until mixture comes to a boil.
9. Then you close lid and bring pressure to 1st red ring (low pressure) over high heat.
10. This is when you adjust heat to stabilize pressure at 1st red ring and cook for 7 minutes.
11. Furthermore, you remove from heat and use Cold Water Release Method (or better still quick release method recommended by your manufacturer).
12. Finally, you stir in Parmesan cheese.

Pressure Cooker Tomato Lentils with a Kick in 20 Minutes!

Ingredients

Servings 4-6

One stalk celery, chopped (you should use it all from stem to leaf)

One medium onion (chopped)

Extra virgin olive oil

1 tablespoon of curry powder

1 cup of lentils (not pre-soaked)

One medium green pepper (not red, it comes out strangely sweet!)

8 ounces chopped tomatoes

Salt

Pepper

Directions

1. First, you add a dash of olive oil in your pre-heated pressure cooker and soften the onion, celery and pepper.
2. Then when the whole mix is softened, add a can of chopped tomatoes.
3. After that, you stir well and add salt and pepper and the curry to taste (for me I put in 1 Tablespoon for just an extra kick of flavor).
4. At this point, you add the lentils into the pan (NOTE: If the lentils were a heaping cup, then you should add two of water).
5. After adding the water, you stir and close the pressure cooker.
6. Raise the flame to high until it starts to hiss.
7. This is when you put the flame to low and wait 20 minutes.
8. Finally, you open your pressure cooker by releasing the vapor.

Mom's Favorite Dalia for Breakfast

Ingredients

Servings 2-3

2 ¾ cups of water

1 green chili (slit)

1 ½ teaspoons of cumin seeds

3 cauliflower florets

1 medium tomatoes (chopped)

1 tablespoon of fresh green peas

4 sprigs of fresh curry leaves (washed and torn)

1 cup of Bulgar wheat (i.e., Dalia, the fat variety)

2 onions (chopped)

1 teaspoon of mustard seeds

3 tablespoons of chopped fresh coriander leaves

10 French beans (washed, ends trimmed and chopped)

1 tablespoon of chopped carrot

1 ½ teaspoons of salt (to taste)

2 tablespoons of oil

Directions

1. First, dry roast the Dalia in a wok until lightly brownish in appearance and it smells aromatic.
2. After which you remove from flame and transfer to a plate.
3. After that, you heat oil in the same wok.
4. Then once hot, add cumin and mustard seeds.
5. Allow to splutter and once they stop spluttering, add curry leaves, green chili and onions.
6. At this point, you stir-fry until the mixture smells aromatic and the onions are lightly browned.
7. Furthermore, you add coriander leaves and mix well.

8. After that, you fold in the veggies, salt and tomato; mix again.
9. This is when you stir in about 2 tablespoons of water to prevent the mixture from sticking to the bottom of the wok.
10. Then you cook on medium flame for 5 minutes.
11. In addition, you fold in the roasted Dalia and mix thoroughly.
12. After which you add water and then transfer the whole mixture to a pressure cooker.
13. Then you cover and pressure cook for 2-3 whistles.
14. This takes about 5 minutes, after which you switch off the gas, and then let the Dalia cook in its own steam inside the cooker for about 2-3 minutes.
15. Finally, after 3 minutes, remove from cooker, garnish with coriander leaves and serve hot.
16. Enjoy!

S'more Chicken

Ingredients

Servings 4

2 tablespoons of butter

Minced garlic

½ cup of soy sauce (preferably Mr. Yoshida's Gourmet Sauce tastes best)

½ teaspoon of nutmeg

6 -8 pieces of meaty chicken

One sliced onion

One cup of water

¼-½ teaspoon of salt

⅛ teaspoon of pepper

Directions

1. First, you brown meaty chicken pieces in butter with sliced onion and minced garlic.
2. After which you place browned chicken and onions in pressure cooker.
3. After that, you dump remaining ingredients over chicken.
4. At this point, you heat on high until pressure cooker top starts to rock, then reduce heat to medium-high.
5. Then you cook for 15 minutes.
6. Remember, it can also be simmered on the stovetop.
7. When serving, serve over rice with sauce.

Pressure Cooker Brown Rice

Ingredients

½ teaspoon of salt

2 cup of brown rice (I prefer short grain)

2 ¾ cups of water

Directions

1. First, combine the rice, water and salt in the pressure cooker pot.
2. After which you lock the lid in place and select High Pressure and 22 minutes' cook time.
3. Then when beep sounds turn off pressure cooker and use a natural pressure release to release pressure (approximately 20 minutes).

NOTE: If you're in a hurry you can use a Natural Pressure for 10 minutes, followed by Quick Pressure Release.

4. Finally, when valve drops, carefully remove lid tilting it away from you.
5. Then you fluff rice with a fork.

Pressure Cooker Ham and Beans with Spinach

Ingredients

Servings 8

8 cups of water

2 teaspoons of onion powder

2 dried bay leaves

1 (about 10 ounce) package frozen chopped spinach

Fresh ground black pepper (to taste)

1 lb. of dried great northern beans

1 lb. of ham

½ teaspoon of garlic powder

1 pinch of crushed red pepper flakes (because I put that in almost everything!)

1 dash of nutmeg

Directions

1. First, you add washed, sorted dry beans to pressure cooker with the water.
2. After which you cut ham into bite size chunks and add all seasonings.
3. After that, you set to HIGH pressure for about 20 - 25 minutes.
4. Then you use quick release method to release steam.
5. At this point, you stir in spinach and nutmeg. Heat through.

NOTE: My cooker has a "Keep Warm" setting that I leave it on till serving time.

6. It is great with crusty bread or cornbread!

Brandied Applesauce
Ingredients

Servings 10 Yield 5 cups

¾ cup of dark brown sugar

⅓ cup of brandy (preferable applejack)

1 pinch of nutmeg

1 pinch of ground ginger

½ (1/2 lemon) tablespoon of lemon zest

4 lbs. granny smith apples

½ cup of apple cider

2 cinnamon sticks

1 pinch of ground cloves

1 ½ (1/2 lemon) tablespoons fresh lemon juice

Directions

1. First, you peel, core, and quarter the apples.
2. Then in a pressure cooker, combine all the ingredients and cook at high pressure for 2 minutes.
3. After that, you let pressure release naturally (NOTE: it'll take 10 to 20 minutes), then remove cinnamon sticks and coarsely chop the apples; alternatively, puree the apples if you prefer a smoother texture.
4. At this point, you taste and adjust sweetness and flavorings.
5. Finally, you set aside to cool, then cover and refrigerate.

Chicken and Tomato Rice Soup

Ingredients

Servings 6

24 ounces of boneless skinless chicken breasts

3 carrots (peeled and sliced ¼ inch thick)

1 teaspoon of dried thyme

4 cups of chicken stock

1 ½ teaspoons of salt

2 celery ribs (sliced 1/4 inch thick)

1 tablespoon of olive oil

1 yellow onion (finely chopped)

3 garlic cloves (minced)

1 cup of long grain rice

1 (about 28 ounce) can diced tomatoes

1 teaspoon of black pepper

¼ cup of fresh parsley (chopped)

Directions

1. First, you pre-heat pressure cooker on the Brown setting.
2. After which you dice chicken into bite-size pieces.
3. After that, you add the olive oil to the pressure cooker and brown the chicken pieces briefly, seasoning with salt and pepper.
4. Then you add the onion, carrots, celery, garlic and thyme; sauté for 2 to 3 minutes.
5. At this point, you stir in the rice, and pour in the stock and tomatoes.
6. Furthermore, you season with salt and pepper to taste.
7. After which you lock lid in place, and cook on HIGH for 8 minutes.
8. This is when you reduce the pressure with the quick-release method, and carefully remove the lid.
9. Finally, you add the parsley, adjust seasoning if needed and serve.

Thai Chickpeas

Ingredients

Servings 8-10 Yield 8-10 cups

3 cups of low-fat coconut milk

¾ lb. of sweet potato (peeled and cut into 1 inch chunks)

1 tablespoon of curry powder

1 teaspoon of fresh grated ginger

½ cup of fresh basil (minced)

1 tablespoon of soy sauce (it is optional)

1 (about 16 ounce) package chickpeas

1 teaspoon of minced garlic

1 cup of fresh plum tomato (coarsely chopped)

1 tablespoon of curry paste

¼ cup of fresh coriander, minced (NOTE: you can also use dried seeds or powder)

20 prunes (chopped)

Directions

1. First, you soak the chickpeas overnight or use the "quick soak" method (NOTE: boil the chickpeas 2 minutes, then soak for 2 hours).
2. After which you drain and rinse the chickpeas.
3. Then in the pressure cooker, combine the chickpeas, coconut milk, garlic, sweet potatoes, tomatoes, curry powder, curry paste, ginger, and coriander.
4. After that, you lock the lid in place.
5. Furthermore, over high heat, bring to high pressure and cook for 18 minutes.
6. After which you allow the pressure to come down naturally (NOTE: If the chickpeas are not tender, either return to high pressure for a few more minutes or replace but not lock the lid and simmer until the chickpeas are done).
7. Finally, you add the basil, prunes, and soy sauce (if desired) to taste as you break up the sweet potatoes and stir to create a thick sauce.

Fava Bean Soup

Ingredients

Servings 2

1 tablespoon of olive oil

5 sprigs of fresh thyme

1 large yellow onion (minced)

½ lemon (juice of)

1 cup of dried fava beans (hulled)

6 garlic cloves

2 bay leaves

4 cups of water

1 teaspoon of salt (or better still more to taste)

Directions

1. First, you sauté onions.
2. After which you add everything (except lemon) to a pressure cooker.
3. Then you cook for 30 minutes.
4. At this point, you adjust water to taste.
5. Finally, you add ½ lemon (juiced).

Esau's Pottage
Ingredients

Servings 4

1 tablespoon of salad oil

Water (to cover)

2 (about 1/4-inch slice) onions, sliced

1 ½ cups of stewed tomatoes (about 15oz)

½ cup of diced celery (I just slice)

½ cup of diced parsnip (slice)

2 cups of water

½ cup of dried lentils

1 teaspoon of salt

¼ cup of salad oil

1 lb. ground lamb (NOTE: since it can be hard to find ground lamb I've thrown in a couple of shoulder chops and shredded them)

½ cup of sliced carrot

½ cup of diced green pepper

1 teaspoon of salt

½ teaspoon of black pepper

Directions

1. First, you mix together and soak overnight: Lentils oil, salt and water to cover.
2. After which you drain and discard liquid next day. (NOTE: I have also eliminated this entire step without a problem).
3. After that, you heat Pressure Cooker and add remaining ingredients along with the lentils.
4. At this point, you pressure cook for 20 min and let pressure drop on its own.
5. NOTE: I usually use more veggies and it comes out almost like a stew instead of a soup.

6. Remember, that the parsnips really help to make this so try to include them.

Pressure Cooker Split Pea and Ham Soup

Ingredients

Servings 6-8

8 cups of water

1 onion (diced)

2 celery ribs (diced)

Sherry wine (it is optional)

1 lb. of dried split peas

1 small ham bone (or better still 1 lb. ham, chunks)

2 carrots (diced)

1 ½ teaspoons of dried thyme

Directions

1. First, you fill pressure cooker with water and other ingredients, except Sherry.
2. After which you make sure the pot is no more than half full.
3. After that, you put lid on cooker, place rocker (if model has one) on vent pipe and bring to high pressure.
4. Then when at correct pressure start timing for 20 min.
5. At this point, you let cooker release steam naturally.

NOTE: If you using a pork bone, in suggest you remove and pull all meat off and add to soup.

6. Furthermore, you adjust salt to suit your taste at this point.
7. After that, you serve with a splash of Sherry if you wish.
8. Note: feel free to start this recipe with frozen pork hock by first covering bone with 8 cups water and pressure cook as directed above for about 30 min.
9. Then cold water release pressure and add the remaining ingredients.
10. Finally, you replace lid, bring to pressure and time for 10 more minutes.
11. Allow the pressure to naturally drop.

Lamb Chops Rosemary
Ingredients

Servings

½ cup of chopped green pepper (it is optional)

1 teaspoon salt (pinch pepper)

1 ½ cups of tomato juice or better still 1 (about 14 ounce) can chopped tomatoes

6 large lamb chops, trimmed (cheap cuts, chump or forequarter)

2 medium onions (sliced)

1 tablespoon of fresh rosemary (or better still ½ teaspoon dried rosemary)

Directions

1. First, in a heavy fry pan, fry the chops in a little oil until brown.
2. After which you add pepper and onions, stir around, add everything else and cover and simmer for about 30 minutes.

NOTE: if the sauce is too thin, I suggest you turn to high and take the lid off for a minute or two.

3. It can be done in a casserole or crock pot.
4. At this point, you make sure you trim off all the fat, or put in fridge for the night and get the fat off the next day, and re-heat.

Corned Beef and Cabbage/Pressure Cooker

Ingredients

Servings 6

2 bay leaves

Horseradish sauce (it is optional)

3 garlic cloves (quartered)

3 peeled and quartered turnips (preferably any additional veggies you enjoy)

2 ½ lbs. of point cut corned beef brisket

1 head cabbage (cut into 6 wedges)

4 cups of water

4 carrots (cut into 3 inch pieces)

6 peeled and quartered potatoes

Directions

1. First, you pour water into pressure cooker.
2. After which you add brisket; over high heat, bring water to a rolling boil.
3. After that, you skim residue from surface.
4. Then you add garlic and bay leaves and secure lid.
5. Furthermore, over high heat, bring to high pressure.
6. After that, you reduce heat to maintain pressure and cook 1 hr. 15 minutes.
7. At this point, you release pressure according to manufacturer's directions and remove lid.
8. This is when you add vegetables to brisket and liquid, stirring gently.
9. In addition, you secure lid abed over high heat, bring steam to high pressure.
10. After which you reduce heat to maintain pressure and cook 6 minutes.
11. Finally, you release pressure according to manufacturer's directions.
12. Then you remove lid.
13. Serve with horseradish sauce.

Good Ol' Southern Soup Beans for Pressure Cooker

Ingredients

Servings 8-10 Units US

1 ham hock (preferably salt pork, ham bone, or other salty pork)

1 garlic clove (minced)

6 cups of hot water

1 lb. of dried beans (pinto preferred, but almost anything will work, my school cafeteria always made them with navy beans)

1 small onion (chopped)

1 tablespoon of butter (or better still 1 tablespoon bacon grease)

Directions

1. First, you follow directions on bean bag for presoaking the beans.
2. After which you drain and rinse beans, sit aside.
3. Then in the pan melt butter (or bacon grease) over medium heat.
4. After that, you cook onions and garlic until soft and lightly brown.
5. At this point, you add beans, ham hock, and water to pressure cooker.
6. Put on lid and seal and bring heat up to high.
7. Furthermore, once pressure has been reached, reduce heat to low and cook for 30 minutes.
8. After which you remove the pressure cooker from heat and release the pressure with a quick release method.
9. Then you remove the cover and test beans for doneness.

NOTE: If necessary you cover and return the pot to pressure and cook for another 5 minutes.

10. In addition, you remove the ham hock from the soup.
11. After that, you discard the skin and bones.
12. This is when chop the remaining meat and add it back to the soup.
13. Finally, you season with additional salt and pepper if necessary.
14. When serving, you serve hot with crumbled corn bread

Andy's Spicy Potato Soup

Ingredients

Servings 8 Yield 12 cups

1 medium onion (chopped)

3 (about 8 ounce) cans tomato sauce

2 cups of corn (fresh or frozen)

½ teaspoon tabasco hot pepper sauce

1 lb. of ground beef

4 cups of water

4 cups of potatoes, 1/4 inch cubed (0.5cm)

2 teaspoons of salt

1 ½ teaspoons of ground black pepper

Directions

1. First, you brown beef and onion well, drain off excess grease.
2. After which you add remaining ingredients.
3. Then you bring to a boil, then simmer for about 1 hour or until potatoes are cooked.

NOTE: make sure you freeze well.

Pressure Cooker Beef Stew

Ingredients

Servings 4

½ teaspoon of salt

1 lb. lean beef (cubed)

½ cup of beef broth

2 tablespoons of minced garlic

½ cup of chopped carrot

2 tablespoons of tomato paste

1 tablespoon of brown sugar

Salt and pepper

¼ cup of flour

¼ teaspoon of dry mustard

1 ½ teaspoons of olive oil

½ cup of chopped onion

2 cups of diced potatoes

1 (about 14 ounce) can tomatoes, undrained

2 tablespoons of balsamic vinegar

1 ½ teaspoons of thyme

2 bay leaves

Directions

1. First, you mix flour, salt, and dry mustard in a bag.
2. After which you add beef and shake to coat.
3. After that, you heat oil in pressure cooker; brown beef pieces.
4. Then you add broth; bring to a boil.
5. Furthermore, you add all remaining ingredients.
6. After that, you lock the pressure cooker lid in place and bring to high pressure over high heat.

7. Cook for about 12 minutes.
8. Finally, you release the pressure, remove bay leaves before serving.

CONCLUSION

Thanks for reading through this book; if you follow judiciously the recipes outlined above, you will improve your health without effort.

Remember, the only bad action you can take is no action at all.

www.ingramcontent.com/pod-product-compliance
Lightning Source LLC
Chambersburg PA
CBHW081726100526
44591CB00016B/2521